Many
Colors
Of
Love

poems by
Sherman Cohen

Cover art and typesetting by John Vincent Palozzi

ISBN-13:
978-1480238183

ISBN-10:
148023818X

Published by
PPB Press
Lake Worth, Florida

Contact Sherman Cohen at:
manycolorsoflove@gmail.com

Dedication

This book is dedicated to Mikki,
who gave birth to the words.
I simply nurtured them until
they were old enough to speak.

Rainbows

I have envisioned one of man's most powerful emotions
as a multicolored rainbow containing various shades
depicted by the multifaceted power of love

I have seen the wonders of it resulting in pain
as well as the pleasures associated with this human drive

It has been used wisely, foolishly, and passionately
with either an arrow or a heavy hammer to the heart

The Author

Contents

Preface: by J. Peter Bergman

In the poem "Eternal" Sherman Cohen relates a timeless illusory factor universally experienced by those who pay attention to their own lives: the impossible task of identifying that moment when we first fall in love. "It is not stationary," he writes, "it moves with the moment." So it is with this book of his. I pick it up and read a few pages, then put it down to take on a more mundane task and when I return to the place where I left the book it has moved somehow to a different part of the room and when I open it to where I left off reading I am not where I thought I would be upon restarting.

That magical sense of his work exists and cannot be defeated. In short spurts of delicate poetry he examines the various shades of love and the shadows cast in those subtle colors. He gives his heart away in some poems and protects his loins in others (read "Stuck"; read "Too Late"). He overturns passion and exposes the child's urgency to become a man (read "Passion's Victim"; read "First Time"). He reminisces like Kurt Vonnegut and predicts like H.G. Wells read "Old Orchard Beach"; read "Now or Never").

Sherman always surprises in much the way O'Henry could at the end of a tale, with subtle humor and with human qualms. He works with the short phrase, the simple thought that carries extra weight in its simplicity. His tiny poem "Divorce" says more about separation within the human condition in only seven lines than Mary Oliver says in her early poem "The Fence" which, in thirty-two lines, divides thoughts along with people and their purposes. Sherman Cohen takes the concept into the personal, deep inside, and reveals the fence inside such a situation and its ultimate loss.

The poems in this volume run the complete gamut on the topic of love. There are moments of violence and moments of solace, instances of an overwhelmed heart, memoirs and projections and the internal narrative straight from the soul. To read this book from beginning to end is essential, but then to pick it up, open it at random and always find the right poem to suit your mood, to bathe your need, is extraordinary. I encourage him to continue exploring my heart and my body and my mind with his musings on his own life experiences.

J. Peter Bergman
Edna St. Vincent Millay's Steepletop
September 21, 2012

Writer, journalist, and artist Peter Bergman is the Executive Director of the Edna St. Vincent Millay Society.

Born in New York City and educated at Queens College, Julliard and the New School, Bergman spent a decade working in New York for the Rogers and Hammerstein Archives of Recorded Sound at the New York Public Library and Museum at Lincoln Center.

Bergman's own published work includes a recent series of plays dealing with real people in Pittsfield, MA, in the 1870s and 1940s.

Bergman received the Charles Dickens Award for <u>Counterpoints</u>, a collection of short stories published by The Digital Hand Press that also published his poetry collection, <u>A Versifier's Childish Garden Gleanings</u>.

He continues to write an arts and fiction website.

To Vincent

Your verse runs wild, sometimes restricted by margin
while I struggle for survival, unbridled by established rules

Alas, my words turn pale next to your vibrant colors

I look to you for even mild inspection, as I suffer so
in my prison of low station and frozen tongue

If you could but drop crumbs of bread along your trail
so I might follow step by step, the path you mark for me

dedicated to poet, Edna St. Vincent Millay

Rhyme and Reason

Can a poet's words mark a painting that, when touched,
can describe the essence of beauty contained
within the margins?

Such a challenge confronts me as I place my pen
to the canvas you have prepared. Am I so arrogant
that I may presume it possible to describe you by
the nature of art alone?

Can I mark the moment as you exist in my world?
I can only brush the surface as I pass, for I am rendered
powerless to create.

I shall compose on the back of each page within the
book of my life. Every line symbolized by the imprint
of your touch. I write of you between the breath of my life
and, thereafter, my words inadequate. Should I have the
power to cultivate the ground where you stand,
an exquisite flower would blossom
and then pale beneath your blush.

I shall not predict the words that form my last sentence.
There will be no final tribute, just the ongoing rhythm
of my pulse in time with yours, without rhyme nor reason.

Speechless

My pen belongs to you
The ink drawn from wells of great loves
gone before

Left behind closed gates
swept away by
moon and stars to spread
ecstasy upon your pillow

As my words are placed
with precision so that nothing is missed
not one dot of passion

All lines joined by the
last sentiment
to the first words of
unconditional love

I am not adequate
of speech to touch you
enough with the needed words

Rather I place these
intending to reveal myself
praying you shall
respond in like

When the ink is long dry
my words shall yet
be moist
for my love for you
is eternal

The Dance

Between us there is space for us to reach
across, to hold, to feel another
heart beating in tune

Though I try to match your rhythm
you dance a waltz while
I dance the tango

Each hears a different tune
as we slide across the dance floor
wearing our costumes

Me, in tight satin pants and red
cummerbund wrapped around
a soft silk shirt with flared sleeves
my hair black and slick

You, gowned in light lace, the color
of spring lilacs, as your diamond
necklace sways with the music
broadcast by white suited musicians

Sadly we stumble and trip
awkward as we try to blend as one
in perfect time

Before midnight we kiss
lips barely touching
both aware that we must
seek new partners

I cannot dance the waltz
You will not learn the tango

Memory

remember what you forgot

perhaps you caught up to your passion's pride
looking at yourself at that shiny wall that
reflects only angles losing all perspective

she looked good for a moment maybe two
her imperfect mouth that curved on one
corner when you ranted on and pissed her off

when she left there was no one to clean it up
you and your hubris spilled all over the floor

so you are alone now without a mop and pail

Sun Rain and Wind

the sun caresses your aura
velvet holding a diamond display

rain falls, drops turning
colored confetti
surrounds your portrait

wind whispers secrets
transports you to
softer places

river kisses your toes
rushes through
leaving purple stones

moon hides in your pocket
glow lighting dreams
with your smiles

stars shine at sunrise
a map for the journey
sunset awaits you

Timeless

Time has no passion
It moves from day to day uncaring, unfettered
by animate objects

The marking of it is man's invention
for we choose to measure our lives in
increments of days, months, and years
As we count off, we record the
wrinkles by falling short
of ambitions

If there is a moment
when upon reflection, there arises
thoughts of falling short, extend
your arms and touch those who have
walked with you, and felt the love

Although your body has changed in
the process of living, your shadow
has not. It has simply grown taller
to cover the blemishes along the way

Do not use numbers as your milestones
Welcome the future in terms
of the joy awaiting you, measured by
the timeless pleasure of being

Hope

She stands with others
Elbow to elbow
Ladies of the day
Wishing on a dream
To fall from the sky
A day with bright visions
From the mundane journey
From the daily rising sun
To a sunset of hope

Now the moment!
Screams of joy
Expectations

The launching point
A second of silence
The toss!
A rainbow of color
Bound with ribbon
Sailing high
Against the sun

It falls towards her
A sudden breeze diverts
Other hands retrieve
Another's wish is true

The wedding party leaves
She stands alone
With no bouquet
Just rice in her hair

Balloons

The first balloon floats upwards
dancing with the wind
the second joins in fancy flight
whispering
his departure

She releases another and another
to the sky-god
to salute
his life

Free floating careless
as he lived
dry eyes follow flight and damn
that he left smoldering
fire behind

The last balloon leaves earth
searching welcome
for his soul

No tears wet the earth
where his body
waits redemption

Illusion

She sits upright, as though
on a throne, dictating her order
to the nervous waiter. Elegance
personifies her persona, while
highlighting the soft velvet of
a celebrity status

To the small alcove across the
room, my retinas alert the zoom
lens, the distance between our tables
becoming a geometric possibility

With poet's license I envision
myself gliding across the dimly
lit restaurant gathering her charms
and beauty, all in a moment of magic

Her scent now coats my lungs
with a sweet flavor of chocolate
sugar as my breath inhales
savoring each grain

Her cats eyes, Grecian nose, the
sensuous mouth and confident
countenance, although framed
and frozen, are still animated

A flow of auburn hair illumined by
sun, shimmers beneath her hat,
wide brimmed and painted with
violet emblems, announce perfection

A draping designers dress clings
close, streaming royal purple silk
with silver accents, a photograph
of style

One shoe planted firmly, another
hangs loosely, held by a nonchalant
toe keeping time to my heartbeat

She looks up at me with parted
lips, revealing a dark green leaf
of spotted spinach firmly glued
between her two front teeth

Dinner For One

A wine glass saved
and
la fortunato
invites us to dine again

The waiter surgically removes the
fruit's garment, which forms an orange snake
engaging the checkered
tablecloth

Exotic aromas melt miles of years
and tears recall
white truffles on hot risotto
pungent garlic touching the tongue
romancing the night

Village girls sing lonely love songs
as insouciant adolescents
meander by our window
framed by pale flowers

Spicy scampi waits to surprise
while balsamic washes sassy salads
The dark Italian announces dessert
in royal fashion
his deep voice matching the hot espresso

There are perfect nights
when every star illuminates
those in love
Touched by reflection
memory cannot die

She is gone, but our table
is still set for two

Quietus

When we speak, overtones are heard
not the spoken word
and do we speak at all?

Are letters formed on surface skin
but not from deep within
where truth slumbers?

But you could feel beneath my breast
the racing pulse that will not rest
for fear of dying.

I cry in! Tears wet my soul
and break upon the shoal
constrained by quiet tongue.

Say the words, the words, I cry!
Say the words before we die
and all is lost.

The echo of your silence rings.
Repercussions that it brings
leaves us empty urns.

So my love, I turn away.
The reason? That you cannot say
"I love you."

Sex and Reality

You sit here smiling,
    while the coffee gets cold
        and the toast dry

Dry as the bottom of your throat
    when you say you may leave

I don't give a damn, but I won't tell you
    You may change your mind

You're good at that
    Frankly, you're not the same

I married you for your body
    I deserve what I got
Low on sex and high on
        blood pressure

I'm getting out while my skin still sticks
    You sure did your best
        to skin me alive!

Leaving me? Love left long ago.

Shouting Silence

My love lasts in unknown places
In a closet high upon a shelf
In a pillowcase waiting for the wash

Behind a broken wall clock
Behind a sofa's cushion
Behind last year's photograph

Inside a closed novel
Inside an unsung song
Inside a relieved breath

Outside your instincts
Outside the silent voice
Outside an unopened door

Higher than your reach
Higher than rain's first drop
Higher than the compass point

My words paint it
My heart anoints it
My voice shouts it

Still, it has not yet been discovered

Children

I miss the sound of footsteps, sealed
under the lacquer stained flooring
creaking in time to the northeast snow
falling against the frozen ground

I miss the thick scent of syrup sucked from
Maple in the fall, still standing strong
even as her blood was drawn from her trunk
delivering her gift to our Sunday French toast

I miss the sound of rakes scraping the grass
holding dry reds and golds tight against the
pull of the children's chafed hands, trapping
their prey

I miss the burning of the leaves against an
autumn sky, as I recall smoke rings
floating like hollow zeroes, adding up to
the sum of another season

I miss the country ride through the Blue Hills
the sounds of the high pitch of adolescence
picked up by the pure air of the mountain
high above the bottom of morning

I miss the passing of each season, and still
hear the changing voices edging a little
closer to the following year, their tones
slightly lower, their playground expanding
along with a larger shoe size and longer reach

Celebrate

The years have branded your character
not with the hot iron of the cowboy's tool
but with the light of dignity
which has illuminated your
lifeline

Your footprints have been cemented in
each landmark you have crossed
on your way to the next one
leaving a lasting impression behind

Even as you extinguish each candle
your soft breath and pure heart
glide on the soft feet of your
presence

Your touch has extended to many
who acknowledge you as the face
of good, kind and considerate

I have been celebrating you
each morning that I leave our bed
and each night we return to lie together

Pain

First, the sudden sounds of crashing symbols
then, the high pitched scream piercing my eardrums
followed by a deep throbbing creeping up from
the ground, tearing at my bones

A wrenching, pulling of my intestines, bends me
forward and the groaning sound of
ripping ribs, brings me painfully upright
sending unfamiliar electric shock through me

My eyes are stung by a stark white light
as my throat closes, chocking out agony
dried blood clogging my veins, causing my heart
to stop, while my brain freezes into icy denial

All this seems as pleasure when compared to your
words announcing your love for another, leaving
my devotion to drown in the deep waters of despair

Stuck

He looks at his watch though he knows the time
It never stops running
His fingers drum across the desk
He peeks through
Beyond the beyond the dream sleeps
He slumbers along
There are no persons spending his future
She is not here
She has faded like a shadow under the light
He is glued to the sanctity
He moderates yesterday's conversations
His part is brief
She has colored in his silhouette in black
The portrait is stored
Unanswered messages wait in the dark

Reaching Back

Where time has fled, shall I
follow, to chase the
dreams left behind
though not in body but
in my mind?

Encourage dream to take
me there
and suit my armor for me
to wear
against the storm
that I may bear.

I shall walk, shoes wet
with dew
with outstretched arms to
reach for you
and wrap the joys with
rainbow's glow
and bring them forth from old
to new.

I know our futures cannot
speak
but through my porous past
they leak
so I will grasp them in my heart
and through the darkness I shall seek.

Sherman Cohen   31

Saturday Evening

"Madame dines alone tonight?"
I'm sure he'll be here soon.
"Perhaps a glass of wine, Madame?"
I'm sure he'll be here soon.

....

"Duck L'orange for two tonight,
the special of the house."
Perhaps a sherry, while I wait,
I'm sure he'll be here soon.

....

"Another glass, perhaps some rolls?"
I'm sure he'll be here soon.
The menu please, while I wait,
I'm sure he'll be here soon.

....

"For dessert we have glaze`,
just the perfect touch."
I think I'll wait.
He'll be here soon.
Besides, I've had too much.

....

"Another cup of tea, Madame?
The hour's getting late."
Just bring the check, if you please,
I've decided not to wait.

The Closet

Come on out
It's dark in there

> *I can't*
> *I'm afraid*

Don't be
The sun's out

> *They'll laugh*
> *They'll hurt me*

What about Joseph
He's out here

He loves you
He'll marry you

> *Are you crazy*
> *Two men*

It's o.k. I promise
It's changed

Open the door
Joseph's waiting

You can come out now

Faded Youth

He feels the same
   the years have not changed
   the texture of his body
   his familiar scent triggers
   emotions dulled by separation
The treasure of first love hidden in a dark corner

Pressing her face to his
   she murmurs sensuous sounds
   soft hairs on his quiet chest
   engage her bosom as if in
   rapturous response
Old feelings turning young as she reminisces

She yearns to return to the magic land
   of innocence where first encounter sleeps
   in warm embrace, uncaring, unfettered
   by worldly worries and life's impositions
   that now demand her day
Mellow sensations sleep with the past

The fresh color of youth
   stained and faded by disenchantment
   matches the dullness in his eyes
   his stare giving no measure of feeling
   no signal, no sight, no connection
To the past fast fading

Saddened she places the furry
   memory in the closet corner
   where Teddy joins dressless dolls
   and broken toys and other childhood sounds
   that speak in whispers
From her past fast fading

Alice's Tea

Here we sit with Alice's tea
eyes gazing at she
she gazing at me

Noiseless words, spoken in sign
I, holding her hand
she, grasping mine

Memory's song, echoing tune
composing the notes
while stirring her spoon

Holding now, forgetting the past
sipping our tea
making it last

Soon she will leave, I, never to see
wonderful Alice
sipping her tea

Flesh and Blood

SON:
what sacrifice
you make when
you give that
hand to me?

FATHER:
no sacrifice,
for that hand
is your flesh
as well as mine.

SON:
it attaches your
arm, not mine.
how can that be?

FATHER:
for you are my
child and there
is no distinction
between us.

SON:
I bleed not
when you are
wounded.

FATHER:
for I would not
have you suffer
the pain.

The Year Before This

Like a fallen elephant
held to the ground
by the weight of itself
I cannot rise to touch the truth

Face to face with your lie
I ignore the signs
and reach to touch
the hem of your body
stroking material
searching for answers
beneath the fabric

Last year was different –

Grains of sand clung to your lashes
fastened by tiny tears
which formed against the
onshore winds off Nauset Beach

We were feathers, floating carefree
dancing in unison, separated
by a minuscule margin

You promised love's music
Now the earth moves down
along with the cacophonous
non-melodic notes of your lie

I refuse to listen and will die
with the memory played
against the ribs over my heart

Present Tense

The uncertainty of soon,
and its sibling later, makes
me wonder about tomorrow.
Sometimes I feel I'm standing
in a puddle, one foot wet, the
other crying for help. I gaze at
the sky, dark clouds now
turning ominous, for fear of
lightening striking me down.

Then, as you usually do when
my life is in of need salvation,
your voice of assurance turns
the dark clouds to puffy white
pillows that float to your music.

Any concerns about the future
dissolve, as I step onto dry
land, leaving my muddy shoe
with my doubts, drowning in
the puddle.

Sooner and later
become one dimensional
as I am always
in the moment
when you are present.

Too Late

I was going to call
I really was
Pick up the phone
The line was dead

I was going to tell you
I was going to tell you face to face
Meet you at the corner
But the corner was dead

I was going to tell you last night
I was going to show you
Show you love
But you already left town

Joy

The search goes on without looking
It's just there, like a nicotine fix
unsatisfied with stale status
restless with what is
an animal-like instinct
a natural longing

It often changes color and shape
I feel it's presence when least unexpected
A surprise gift on an ordinary day

I had met a girl named Joy
I could never extract her name
It hid in the recesses of body matter
I believe it remains in her signature

I recall an experience of pure Joy
It came with the birth of my daughter
She arrived in the expected package
Pure Joy was revealed
when I opened it!

Lifelove

Were I to walk this earth alone
mark the clouds and mark the sky
wonder at the quarter moon
breathe the seagulls passing by
taste the sounds of all that's sweet
feel the spring time cool my feet
but not my lifelove to meet
to thaw a January freeze
then all to pass would pass for naught
and all that passed would be forgot

But I have walked a wider trail
enough of space to stretch my arms
to hold the hand that set the sail
that made the rough sea soft and calm

My lifelove keeps my purpose strong
inspires me each waiting day
though shadows now grow ever long
she causes them to go their way

And towards the end, when I look back
to listen for the drum and fife
I'll know true love I did not lack
because of her throughout my life

High View From A Rock Seat

I love the high view
from the rock seat
next to the eagle's nest
above the lake

I can see silence and hear
the bear mating
red throat choking ecstasy

I breathe better here
my nostrils
dilate and suck in pure ice
I exhale joy

Peace finds me here
late morning, leaning
back against the strong pine
I cannot find this
in our double bed

I have one foot on the mountain
and one leg in the lake

The spread is killing me

Department Store

Hired because she resembles
the scent of expensive perfume

I can neither sleep
nor eat after seeing her

My heart drops to my knees
my nerves approach
possessed by obsession

Speech smothered beneath
my tongue

I ask for
after shave lotion

She replies
"I have nothing for you"

Smoke and Mirrors

It comes from swirling smoke
yet burns not the leaf

The fool who offers joke
defies a true belief

The rabbits disappear
to drown in witches brew

First there and then to here
what's old becomes what's new

So when it reappears
be kind, for love is near

Hiding Places

Who I am lies behind
the skin I'm in

Lies beyond
the play I act

Hides behind
stadium eyes

Hides beyond
my lies of fact

Stands behind
a velvet curtain

Preaches gospel
though uncertain

Who I am
God only knows

Parts of me
revealed in prose

Look for me
in every space

Before I'm lost
without a trace

Flavors

Savor one at a time
sampling the taste of each
year, coating palates with
sweet memories

Hold them aloft
balancing the vision
against a perfect sky

Three hundred sixty five
flavors, one for each day
climbing, floating
while we hold hands
beneath a soft blanket

Select one and allow it
to stand alone
as it becomes a new experience
to share again

They are all contained in
your gift box, wrapped
each day with a new ribbon

Soldier's Reward

A crack in the glass mars the picture
Her smile cries at me
I recall the kiss long gone

Image of the moment
measured by the broken
clock losing time
Oriental eyes mock black sky
the soldier holds her hand
Child of wet fields growing life
beneath her naked feet
Death tramples grass

Spider webs trap hours
The generals separate platoons
and all lovers, forever
His uniform gone

He holds her softly in his heart
Pain freezes his bones
Night offers only a cold blanket
I left you beneath a black sky

Music of The Heart

In the deep recesses of my heart
sleeps lyric
whose prose reaches for music –
to form a song complete

It speaks of love so sweet –
that only pure notes
can blend

Not music for the ear –
the poem must find
your heart
to form a song

Listen for the music –
if not for you
I would be a voiceless word

Black And White

when these colors are mixed
the result is not grey
the colors are black and white
occupying the same space

attracted by osmosis and
the pull of the moon's magnet
two opposites unheeding the
law of the artist's palette

there is not a boundary
there are no borders
the critics wander museums
clicking tongues making judgment

the act of love is not an exhibit
to be admired or ridiculed
it is an emotion free of prejudice
and the opinion of small minds

the canvas is blank
whether black and white
brown or yellow
allow the artist to choose
without prejudice

Permission

I cleaned out his closet
I need permission
He does not answer
He lies beneath the headstone
He was always a quiet man

I cannot open the door
It is closed tight
Cufflinks share space
In my change purse
We bought them in Paris
I don't know where to keep them

I am getting married
It has me by the throat
I cannot breathe
I need permission to breathe
I need his permission

Yesterday I heard his voice
I called back – no answer
Just the sounds of the house
I cannot leave
The door is locked

We join hearts
My new husband
My new life
I'm living behind closed doors
It's my secret

I wait for his permission
But he is silent

Flame

As I match line to rhyme, and try the same each time
I sadly fall behind the tempo of the music's metaphor
My sounds but mutter and I can only stutter warbled word

I light love candles, both tops and bottoms, plant
Them firmly at your footstep, and listen for your rustle
The fires flicker and flame, as I stand guard against wind

Figures of Semetrius

Wormlike veins give truth to lives
born before their history
Perfect bodies so finely tuned
that missing limbs still grasp the
marble waists of lovers

My heart tears loose, searching
behind each shadow
longing to bring forth the
Myth of Prothias
from the ruins

Their arms taken piece by piece
by the Snake of Sarcas
who came from beneath the waters
and embarked on the land to reek
havoc on the city of Tilus

He had destroyed his enemy Prothias,
in a death struggle that shook
the clouds and caused the moon to die
leaving below the heat of his hate

All had withered to small stones
except the lovers in the city of Semetrius
who were frozen in their positions
by a falling star

It is said that Prothias will reappear on
earth to slay the Snake of Sarcas, and then
the statues will gain their limbs
to hold each other in protection
throughout eternity

Liquid Letters

Will the wells run dry?
Only if the iris of my eye
forever loses you.

Will I lose the word?
Only if silence is not heard
above the noise.

Will images I forget?
Only when the sun does not set
in seas of love.

Will love not sustain?
Only when the scent of rain
loses flavor.

Will I ever love you never?
Only when universe forever
loses memory.

Shall these answers be the
prose of my life?
Are the questions too remote,
or do they drink the
words I wrote?

Shunned

My windswept heart joins passing clouds
and I am empty so alone
Mourners wearing sorrow shrouds
vent their anger chill my bone

Their backs are turned to face my face
they walk direction out from me
And so I drift a backward pace
to forget the backs I see

I find myself alone at night
a motion picture in reverse
The shadows part allowing light
projecting image from my purse

For locked within the vaulted heart
now stolen from the present tense
reveals the years that we did part
The picture wounds from that time hence

And so with wounded soul I live
away from those who cause me pain
But long for those who won't forgive
so I can love myself again

Beach Blues

Her toes press each grain of sand separately
and the sun licks the ocean salt
drying the corner of each eye

She inhales the scent of sky
broadcasting letters
shaped by talcum clouds
whispered words
delivered to her heart by the rainbow
every color a soft kiss

The beach empties and she stands
alone
framing his picture in her gallery
while yesterday's voice
tattoos her soul
with memory's promise

Passion's Victim

Beneath skin of crag and crevice
The soft surface is buried

Her lifeline strokes my cheek
I struggle the tide
Dark memory awakens

Her tongue washes her lips
Tasting corners

I am caught in the net
Amber eyes piercing my flesh
Her sweet breath blinds me

I succumb to red passion

My desire its victim
A muddy bottom pulls
I struggle below the surface

Time

Time is but a series of events
held together by a clock
so subtle that one can barely see
the hands in motion

One must reflect and step across
the years reversing time
to the beginning

We should cherish the hours
for providing space
meant for us to enjoy
moments in the time allotted

As we move forward
too often we ignore
the quiet of the
tick tock tick tock

Here hangs the antique clock
moving uninterrupted
pointing out tomorrows
reminding us to share
our love today

Haircut

Saturday's crowd reads the news aloud,
     from Saturday's Post,
while smoky cigars clouds conversation.
     White sheet encases his frame,
     from neck to knees,
locked tight by safety pin.
     (the boy hears only his heart)

The static from the radio predicts
     tomorrow's winners,
while dark men exchange cash,
     then his captor's reassurance
is cut thin by the sudden din
     of the razor.
The burn upon his nape takes toll,
     as he slumps into submission.
A snipping, snapping sound of the
     predator's teeth,
turns shoulders to jelly, while the
     fine filament floats to the floor.

Tight eyes open wide when wet fire
     is applied,
but the barber's brush kisses his tears
     and powder sooths his ears,
while the soft touch of kindness
     pats his head.
He stifles a sniffle when he looks in
     the mirror at the "man" with a whiffle.

Later, when tucked in his bed,
  his father strokes his bristled head,
   and the men of the house
    are forever bonded.

The Promise

Stand on this rocky shore
beneath my dream
and
I will cleanse the air to fill
your heart
with
scents of aliveness
and
joy of the mountain

I shall color your life
with
the richness of the tall pine
and
the hope of a new rose nourished
by
the sweetness of this
Celtic earth

My love
rest with me
and
stay for eternity

The Waiting Game

She waits...
>
> the sound of the antique clock
> design of the ages
> responds to the hanging metronome
> one nervous hand pulling the other
> creeping indefinitely forward

She has waited...
>
> when the promise of his return
> locked in the mirrored cabinet
> next to Dr. Scholl —
> the razor's rust staining her vanity

She waits...
>
> for waiting is before dying
> perhaps life still holds another promise
> and the closed hinge may yet open
> a declaration

She waits...
>
> knowing his return is a dead hope
> killed by too much love given
> with too much love taken

She will wait...
>
> until the last pair of socks
> disappears from his bureau

Mothers and Daughters

My child is bright and new as the
first evening star
Full cheeked she sleeps the dreams
of blank verse

I provide life and she rewards me
with her presence
turning each day page by page
so as I may read the diary
of each year

From sunsuit to snowsuit I mark
the seasons with photos
carefully stored in the
bureau of my heart
The pictures mirror her smiles
with mine

She grows through the years
catching autumn leaves
Summer sand
clings to her toes
while the wind of winter
waits to escort her to spring

Today I bend forward
to match her level
as we walk in cadence
to our music

Tomorrow the daughter
will replace the mother

Andy Warhol

I watch the butterfly alight on
the rusty Campbell Soup can,
and note the disparity.

The Cadillac pulls up besides
the trash can
and the open mouth accepts
garbage from the rich rider.

I wonder about colors that
do not blend,
distinguished by our perception
of the rainbow.

Because she and she are in love

are their colors to be not
included in God's gift
spread across the sky?

Eternal

I cannot find the moment
I first fell in love
When I search it is not
where I put it

It is not stationary
It moves with the moment
It dwells between
heartbeats

It is the same
never changing
since the beginning
always the same

It lives in me
It feeds on your smile
It is aware only of you

There is no measure for it
for
it exists in a timeless dimension

Affection

The word is sometimes used
to avoid love's strong statement

It disguises commitment and
speaks with soft volume

Supporting words can be
used to circumvent the loss of
independence that is the
nature of true love

It is often used as a metaphor
which can easily confuse and
conflict with the listener's
expectation

Affection may thrive on image
translated into a language
misconstrued by the recipient
and not understood by its
originator

True love must be broadcast
with large font to eliminate
the thick veil of doubt

The Muse

Come tap my shoulder
Inspire my words
so I may speak to paper

Words that ink will spread
on parchment
will expire only when time does

Create the magic of
ultimate emotion
so I might pierce the
heart of purpose

Help me transcend
capacities beyond just
eloquent accents

Implant my love into
her sensibilities

Magician

To live with the perfect woman
is pure magic
Concerns that cloud my silent voice
are made to vanish simply
by her quiet command

She watches me with the eye
of a new mother
and pulls rabbits from her hats
amusing my day

My table set colorful scarves
slide from her sleeve
soft silk caressing
my tired face

Nightly her body rests with mine
and mornings bring the
touch of her wand on my heart
bringing forth her joy for
my new day

The curtain remains open
The props stand by
ready to amaze her audience

I sit first row aisle seat
with awe and admiration

Summer Sky

The landscape of her voice
brushed by the summer sun
reaches the top of the
mountain
rising towards the
skywriter's message

Clouds part exposing a
red river rushing to
the brim of an angry
waterfall
plunging to the
bottomless bottom

My eyes project the image
as I gaze upward from
a prone position
flat as the horizontal hope
of rejection
looking for a signal
of reversal

Though I scramble the
alphabet of her message
it remains without
alteration

The oncoming autumn
will change the colors
but the landscape
shall remain the same
for me

Patience

The statue of the lovers
at the water's edge
inhale the scent of lilies
and the boxwood hedge

The graceful birds of spring
instruct the winds to toss
inviting morning dew
from its bed of moss

While rhododendron holds
tight her summer bud
and winter winds freeze
the oozing autumn mud

I shall rest
and reminisce
and wait again
for lover's kiss

The Toothache

He feels the pulsating pain
of an angry tooth, but
cannot extract it from his
fantasy. The throbbing
sounds resonate, filling
his eyes with the sight of
her laughing on her way
out the door. The talk was
short and sweet and the
dismissal caught his
fingers in the rusty hinge
of a relationship doomed.
The pain, so subtle, picked
the broken pieces from his
pockets. Now, resolved to
move along, he vows to
extract the source, and brush
away the debris he still
tastes.

Past Due

Rain slaps against the windowpane
in the steady pattern
of a tap dance
in time with the sting of rejection –
a vinegar against my wounds

Yesterday the sun shone
while a dark horizon
slept on the rim –
when he greeted me with an
unfamiliar smile
I felt a tear in the
seam of the afternoon

How many rendezvous –
how many nights waiting
for the day to chase the loneliness
without him

Hope had survived thriving
on promises made before the
blanket was turned –
before passion smothered
sensibility

It is finished –
like an overdue book
I cannot keep his love
without penalty

First Time

Innocence lost beneath her plaid skirt
wool scratching my eagerness
My clumsy pretense of experience
attempts to imitate only what
my imagination can conjure up

Her breath tastes like Uneeda Biscuits
glued to her braces sharp edges designed
to thwart the French kiss that
I practiced against the bathroom mirror
in anticipation of the great event

She does not moan, like she is supposed to
according to the porno movie
screened at my brother's stag party
She does not gasp or scream according to script
nor does she move any muscle in her
complete body

I think (I am not certain, fifty years later)
I lost my virginity that Sunday afternoon
behind Shapiro's Variety Store

It is quite possible her virginity is still in tact

Final Dance

The bitter wind slips along the lake
With hunched shoulders
feet turned under
I sit dead center
eight inches
above

False promise slides through
the cracks plunging below
lurching and twisting
a distorted ballet
anxious to find a new partner
beneath the icy surface

When summer arrives
I shall wait at the shore

Strolling

where you're going
can I follow
where you're going
can I come
you can follow
I can follow
you can follow
where I'm going

walk beside you
where you're going
walk beside me
where I'm going
hold your hand then
where we're going
hold my hand now
while we're going

hold you closer
where we're going
hold me closer
on the way
arm around you
holds you closer
hold me closer
on the way

can I kiss you
when we get there
you can kiss me
on the way
I can kiss you
while we're going
I can kiss you
when we're there

Fleeting Moments

I see you in a private room
reserved for fleeting moments

A certain smile joins
the subtle movement of your hand
signaling a message

My impatience between
visits as I try to
fill the spaces

My heartbeat keeping time
with the melody
of your laughter

The glow of you
that settles wherever
it visits

I must blot these moments,
before they dry without
your inscription

Dazzled

Glossy and shiny letter
phrases that dithers and dazes
stanzas better and better
music that glows and amazes

I must dazzle and delight you
make you feel faint
stunned by my words
by the pictures I paint

Prove my love
indent and pierce
create a buzz
passion fierce

Can poet's muse
affect my song?
Can words I use
Last a lifetime long?

Shakespeare

I may attend a class, for me to write
better prose than now I know
to raise my work to greater height
to bring my words to where I go

I read Shakespeare through dead
of night
and study Browning's word
to stretch my mind to reach a height
creating verse not heard

Though all my compositions flow
with meter image metaphor
it all means naught unless you know
I write for whom I most adore

My object is improving art
inspiration with magic muse
so to bring forth from my heart
the many angles of my views

Awakening

Sweeten my tears with yours
no salty sting
to blur the cold moon

Cry but refuse recalcitrant
memories their passage
resist the veiled virgin's
voice

When I depart return your love
until it wakes
to embrace another

The day is still
just a quiet quiver as my shadow
passes

Elastic Breaks

Rubber Ribbons
stretch across
and down
a box
of
answered questions

Remove both
to reach
but do not tug

Elastic snaps
and what's inside
can escape
leaving an empty
container

your questions
unanswered

Bernie

I lost my friend today, but he's not gone. As silent as snow falling from a branch, he has found a place not visited by those of us left behind.

I hear his movement. I feel his expressions. I see timepieces carefully stored, companions added at whim. He sings for me. "Getting to know you, getting to know all about you." He is in the back seat of my car and sings to me. He asks me, "Have you got a minute?" Then tells me a funny story. He cries when he watches old movies, letting us know his heart never runs out of compassion.

He is proud. It shows with each carefully chosen uniform. Each necktie, cufflinks, coat, hat, and suited garment, selected for his day's purpose. He departs the premises with aplomb and carefully selected coiffure in place, purchased long before it was fashionable.

He knows everyone and amazes me with his perception. I listen for his animated laugh. I think, Jack E. Leonard or one of the old time comics. His impeccable taste in art, is for arts sake, and I ask him, "Do you have too many?" "Not enough to fill each open space my eyes fall on. Not enough to satisfy my thirst for the beauty to light my world." He adds more life to his life and wastes none, even while he sleeps.

I am in the world he left, searching my brain cells, trying to fertilize each one with fresh memories. Perhaps another vision, another scene will smile my lips, will lift my heart, will moisten my eyes, will bring him to me.

Now, he has left but he is not gone. He no longer lives but he is not dead. I cannot see him, but he is here.

Apology

the waited word
the silent voice
is heard

the touch of the muse
the pulses beat
the healing bruise

the tears now dried
the cheek still damp
the promise tried

the hands now hold
the passion's back
the hearts unfold

Facing North

The temptress offers delicacies
covering
mischief
and misdeeds
of lust

The test has begun
for those with
untrained muscles
and weak
tendencies

The compass pokes
and probes
pushing away –
always
pushing away

It is overwhelming
Even so
I must resist
facing North

New Beginnings

The hazy dream conceals
I must swim through the fog
to reach you

Time sleeps the night
and wakens with me

I shall touch memory
before the flowers wilt
and the well is dry

Where is yesterday?

Unspoken Words

You make my heart so light as though
a feather may be a burden
by its weight

As though the soft cloud weighs heavy
in the sky even after
rain

Like an opening stanza announcing itself
your subtle smile promises
my imagination substance

My breath ripples like the summer sand
of receding tide when I hear
your sweet sound

I see you dressed in nakedness revealing
the blissful bite of
anticipation

The scent of you remains long after your
touch and I am consumed by
its language

Leave me now if only your absence will
remind me of you
while I suffer the exquisite taste
of emptiness

The Easy Path

how easy to live life expected
how easy to follow from birth
how easy to be not rejected
how easy to own manly worth

how easy to sleep undercover
how easy to hold my breath
how easy to act as another
how easy to wait for my death

Widow's Walk

She feels a single strand
glued to her cheek by drying tears
and the memory of him lingers
yet in the room of yesteryears

She thinks of mornings when elbows
rest on the window sill
while they watch the gloom
of night's end

City lamps ceased to light
as quickly as he ceased to live
and she could not forgive
the day for turning black

Beyond the romance of love
they loved one another
and a stronger bond could not be
tied and yet he died

Friends uncomfortable in their
condolence promise her future
but it lies only in the past
and their last happy day

The ceremony over the Yisgadal prayer said
now his catatonic body
rests in her bed

The young widow is old in her new role
and plays it without conviction
her complexion matching her grief

They both shall sleep the long sleep

Sherman Cohen

Divorce

Ma says he's forgotten
He remembers

The horn blows downstairs
He remembered

We spend the day
He does not stay

Night is without him
I remember

First Kiss

I recall our first kiss

It was in my car
a black Plymouth

You were so beautiful
with amber eyes
auburn hair
a certain way about you

I dared you to tussle
my hair
and you did

I always kept it just so
walked towards the wind
so my hair wouldn't blow
and you messed it

I said I would kiss you if you did
and you did!

That was our first kiss

I still feel your fingers
running through my hair

Mission

TO FILL that space selected by God

TO HOLD hands in harmony

TO TRANSLATE language unspoken

TO SEE beauty beyond vision

TO HEAR a voice through silence

TO SHARE the undivided in equal parts

TO WALK abreast in single file

TO JOIN in symphonic sound

TO INHALE the wonder of you

Now Or Never

Too many words to say
nothing

We're running out of time
yesterday died
tomorrow's
a breach birth

We hold back
storing words

Say it now!
tomorrow may
be cancelled

Fresh Flowers

The magician makes the past vanish
and moves to the present
with a slight of hand

The nurse announces her visit
I feel the strength of her devotion
making soft the hard trip ahead

Though I shall also vanish
like the last daylilly of summer
my roots will replenish
and the perennial flower
will blossom

Seasons

The last seagull cracked clams
on the purple rocks
soring and swooping to the song
of the waves

Her footprints were still damp
from the ocean's stain
She left before the dusk
covered our shadows

The summer heat gave way to
loneliness leaving me with
an empty night
I searched the sand for
anything she touched

Now the chill of autumn tugs
urging me to winter's visit
I shall sleep the season
and look for her
next summer

Exit

The roar of engines cannot
drown out the sound of a
river of blood coursing through
not able to wash away the debris
still clinging on

Ten years have passed since
she left on my command, exiting
the same doorway through which
she will return, storming with the
powerful face of revenge rushing
to me in full battle gear

I deserve the ripping wrath as
evidenced by each night of agony
suffered since the dark drive
to the airport

I refuse to excuse my actions to
her or myself as punishment
and when we finally meet I shall
accept her wrath without defense

She comes now!
Forgive me for leaving

The Butcher's Wife

Musical notes dance about her throat
composing a necklace of song
Her green gown screams at the seams
resisting abundant thighs
The diva's arms reach for high C
as the sorcerer's sword
ends act I with a final thrust

Oh, the nights wasted, avoiding Juliet's
sorrow and the white swan
of the lake
when a balcony ticket could be
my permit to pleasure!

The huge man opens act II
with the power of his bass
while the woman's bosom heaves
a heavy sonata

I notice the butcher's wife nearby
and think
I had misjudged this erudite woman
behind the pork and livers
.
Act III transports me from my seat
to the king's throne
My garment turns purple from the dust
of royal guards
Tears touched my soul as the queen
throats her sweet song of departure

Later, beneath the marquee
I long for the music to follow me home
accompanied by
the butcher's wife

Good Boy

Mama says he sat in this chair
watching me sleep. I was so
beautiful that he cried. My eyes
are blue like his. Sometimes I
look at the picture and I think
he smiles when I do.

Maybe he still sits here when
I'm asleep, and watches me and
tells me things about himself.
Mama says "Good boys go to heaven."

I'll be good, and he'll pick
me up and we'll look at
each other, with the same blue eyes.

Differences

We play the same music
and finish together

yet your sharps are my flats —
your majors are my minors

Our chords clash
but still the song is the same song

Our audience listens with
their own perspective

picking at the sounds of
the rhythm sections

keeping their own connection
with the tapping of feet

Let Dizzy and Louie and Mel
inspire your tunes

and live in the company of
those that do it best

Wall Flowers

When they were young at the ball

They sat in chairs along the wall

Now they're old and weathered by

The dance they missed, the music's lie

Free Love

When I took out my subscription
to love, it came with no strings
attached. I received a 30-day
free trial and was promised
daily delivery for this period

The free issue is expiring,
and to renew I must pay the
full price. The high cost causes
me to ponder. During the trial
period the emotions extended
to me by the issuer, were every
thing promised. Now, at renewal
time, I wonder whether the price is
too high to pay, and can I count on
the daily delivery of every issue?

I kept the original subscription
on file, and intend to examine the
conditions more closely. Considering
the high price of love, there may be
other choices less costly, perhaps
more enjoyable. I am now inclined
to purchase a Kindle so I can
download a sample of love —
without penalty

Birth

my words
dried
swept away
by yesterday's
years
fresh letters give
birth from wombs
of memory
lake water dilutes
tastes of salt
images play
over my heart
ribs press
into your soul
pushing back
present tense
fountains of passion
soaking sighing
clinging bodies
now
beyond now

The Color of Water

Like the color of water, which changes under the weather's influence, so your eyes reflect the storm in your heart.

My last letter, written with trembling pen, reflects my rapid pulse fleeing anticipated rejection. I fear my love shall drown in the rough waters of your wrath.

Old Orchard Beach

Babe plays a golden sax
we balance beer mugs
bottom to top
spare change on wet rings
initials scratch posterity
lounge pours watered whiskey
the Canadians come, eh?

We come up from Boston
find strange women, eh?

Babe adopts us
refusing to quit
clutching slippery cliffs
reflection clouds mirror
anxious studs breathe heat
lipstick stains dry lips
sad songs sweep red rouge
smiles hide bad news
she sleeps without night
good times gone bad, eh?

Many Colors of Love

Pisces

I see you in my private room
reserved for fleeting moments
that memory cannot capture

Your certain smile
the subtle movement
the signal of a message

The rush of impatience
the stain of intolerance
the frustration of injustice

My heartbeat keeping time
to the melody of
your laughter

Your eyes of intuition
that pierces the
steel of future

Pisces swimming with Gemini
across years reaching
distant shores

The Picture Book

The summer sun of August
reflects a bright blue sky
complete with memories

White cotton clouds paint
characters crossing bridges
connecting last year to a new
one giving promise

Reflections shimmer and
float marking the decades that
formed the destinations yet to
be determined

Ahead the mysteries of
tomorrows while behind
we leave a picture book
of pleasures

With locked hands and hearts
we move forward to forever

Viewed From the Rear

Stomping on sidewalk lines
she pushes her babies
in rhythm with her sway

Fat red shorts
tight in her left cheek
wrinkled on the right
          and
stained by the burden carried

Last year's hair-do matching
varicose veins and plaid blouse
unglued where belly meets waist
          and
neck greets torso

She is noticed for the infants
and her size extra large
her beauty is not in costume
          but
remains enclosed
          waiting to be disclosed
          by a keen eye
          and a loving heart

Apostrophe Love

May I love you conditionally, with strings attached?
May I pour salt on your wound and apply a band-aid?
May I kiss your ringless finger with sour breath?
Can I not be granted love's promise for my own use?
Can I define true love without contradiction?
Was not my gender decided in the bible's Garden?
Was I not made all powerful to protect and possess?
Must I implore you to let me lead the way I determine?
Do you dare show me one ear and the other to others?
When I press with heated lips why do you resist?
Have I not chosen you above all others?
Do not be ungrateful!

Broken Compass

How can I describe what love
has eyes to see
directed from above
to guide me through to thee

Should reason ask for answer why
though ponder then to search my soul
not even he from mountain high
can wake my dream for me to know

A bursting pulse a heart that yearns
a beckoning from silent mouth
I follow blind the path that turns
with compass magnet drawing south

Sun-clouds warning turning grey
beseeching me to leave my place
demanding that I turn away
and nor to love an empty face

And yet I know the truth is told
but still I cannot turn away
for love is mild and passion bold
and I shall greet the coming day

Roving Eye

Having met many girls
with reference to my prime
and having met many more
from then to present time

I dare say I'm one who has
discerning eye
for pulchritude and attitude
and who what and why

In my endeavors of female type
I've tried to play it safe
ignoring fanfare and feminine hype
selecting wheat from chafe

A difficult and demanding chore
to see through wiles and whims
no matter how often seen before
my recollection dims

When sometimes letting down my guard
the flash of flame burns bright
just then I look in my back yard
when blinded by this light

There you are reminding me
of what I always knew
let all the others simply be
I have the one in you

Lost

Somewhere along the line
perhaps beneath a shading pine
are words not spoke
the truth of them we
did not invoke

Voices heard averted vision
we not aware of decision

Held by passion's heated drip
emotions clenched
in passion's grip

Others whispered silence kept
words intended too inept
to tell us what we should have known

Beneath a drought
dead seeds were sown

The time has come for me to see
the future realistically

Now the facts to me revealed

I cannot love lost love

True love must be sealed

Madelayne

Contemplative melancholy balanced
on a stool
Violins in harmony demeanor seems
quite cool
Oblivious to everything but champagne
in her glass
She glances up legs now uncrossed
and leans against the brass

"Another *bubbly* Charlie please"
holding back the tears
"Tonight you see I'm celebrating
twenty-seven years"

The past becomes the present
when I reminisce and dream
of that young girl so much in love
and all that could have been

Promises on promises our lives
would be entwined
Our futures bound together
so fatefully designed

Instead my friend here I am
drinking up the night
Living out a shallow life
accompanied by trite

It's all baloney Charlie Boy
never meant to be
'Cause twenty seven years ago
Don Juan walked out on me!

Many Colors of Love

Soft Songs

He kisses soft eyelids
The sun rests at the edge of
darkness
A new beginning

Stars nod beneath pillows
Crows commit to
silence
Cacophony now sleeps

Sunrays celebrate ritual
The choir blends love
with heaven

Lovers harmonize.

Quandary

If I could hold the past
and breathe new life
would I live the future
like this
or
would regret drown
in memory's sea?

Can music sound notes
absent from the present?

Can I forgo the past
for this future and
still not lose all in the process?

Yet, I cannot risk the question
for to touch your smile
leaves me no option

Fault

It's just a bruise
He didn't mean it
An accident
I shouldn't have said it
He warned me not to
My fault

I didn't call
The neighbor did
She misunderstood
911 in error
He's a good man
No, he didn't break my nose
I fell
He drinks a little
No harm
Thanks for coming
No problem here
Goodnight
I know he loves me

Forever

listen to my music
the lyric is for you
waltz the song of lovers
sing my song on cue
grasp my face with fingers
hold my smile in mind
see that love not lingers
love me back in kind
match my lips with yours
press your heart to mine
love me just because
what is coarse refine
memorize my eyes
open them to you
fill them with surprise
stretching wide with view

at night I lie awake
and hold the dark in sight
for fear the dream will end
when morning ends the night
so stay with me in song
our music is in view
let's forever last as long
as I shall live for you

Legacy

In the deepest forest of the dark
there sleeps words I have yet to compose

To my children and all whose blood flows
from their blood, and all that sleep in the
welcome beds of God's ceremony, touching
the lives of each branch extending, I invite
you to search your hearts for my truth

Perhaps I shall never find the poetry that yet
eludes me. If not, let this suffice, until you may
stumble upon that secret place in the hidden
forest and all will be revealed. My birth
connected to yours, provides a cord not severed
through which I am attached to each of you

Know that from wherever the source, you shall
always be tied to that heritage, and the
pulse of this extension will be with you always

I love you, not as a word, but with my being

Through words not yet composed, the energy
of my life, and the memory of it, shall be
the metaphor for the poem never recited

Afterwards

Even "afterwards" I shall be writing poems of love

With motion and metaphor I will sing my songs

Sweet melody will fill you as my message pierces your soul
Pretty pictures shall form syllables and light the night
The horizon will explode with a thousand balloons
Colored clouds shall broadcast the scent of your skin

Verse joins songs of doves cooing.
Listen for the voices
They form love sounds from my lips

Made in the USA
Charleston, SC
10 January 2014